GIOVANNI GIULIANI

guide to
SAINT PETER'S BASILICA

Edizioni A.T.S. ITALIA

*We wish to express special thanks to
His Eminence Virgilio Cardinal Noé,
President of the Fabbrica di S. Pietro
for his permission to publish many of
the pictures contained in this book.*

*We are grateful to Dr. Alfredo Maria Daniele Pergolizzi
for his valuable cooperation.*

Editorial:	Frida Giannini
Lay-out and Graphics:	Sabrina Moroni (ATS Italia)
Photography:	Archivio Fotografico della Fabbrica di San Pietro Arturo Mari Istituto Fotografico SCALA K&B News Foto (N. Bonafede) ATS Italia (A. Regoli - C. Tini)
	The publisher will be happy to supply data regarding unidentified picture sources to anyone entitled to such information.
Production and Printing:	ATS Italia - Rome
Printed:	May, 1995
Exclusive distributor:	ATS Italia - Via Francesco Sivori, 6 - Rome - Phone 06/39726079

Foreword

Father Giovanni Giuliani OFM Conv., coordinator of the Volunteer Guides of the Peregrinatio ad Petri Sedem, wrote this book for visitors to St. Peter's Basilica straight from the heart.

If I am not mistaken, he is the first scholar who offers historical, artistic, and cultural information along with spiritual reflections. He draws upon knowledge gained during ten years of guiding pilgrims and visitors around the greatest temple in Christendom, during Holy Years (1975; 1983/84) and ordinary years. But now, under the pontificate of John Paul II, every year is a Holy Year, so great is the pull he exerts on people of all faiths and creeds, be they Catholic or not. Father Giuliani's aim is to present St. Peter's as a true sanctuary, a house of prayer as so beautifully expressed by the Prophet Isaiah: "...mine shall be called a house of prayer for all people" and to help the casual tourist become a real pilgrim.

Some people come to St. Peter's as if it were a museum: they satisfy their curiosity and leave. Perhaps they have learned something new if they are acquainted with art and history, but inside they are untouched.

Those who come to St. Peter's with an open mind and a sincere heart come away changed. Often they go to confession; others, of different faiths want to learn more about the Church.

St. Peter's is the sanctuary of the Faith. Even the most hurried and distracted tourist starts to think more profoundly after hearing our volunteer guides. And it cannot be any other way after realizing that this is where Peter, the first pope, was martyred. Here is the tomb of the man who said to Jesus "Thou art the Christ, the Son of the living God" and to whom Jesus replied "Thou art Peter, and upon this rock I will build my church" (Matt.16:18); "strengthen (the faith of) thy brethren" (Luke 22:32),; "Feed my lambs" (John 21:15).

Ever since the beginning, even during the persecutions, the faithful have come here, even risking their lives. Today, thanks to the mobility made possible by modern transportation, they come in multitudes, from every continent, thirsting for truth.

The Apostle Peter, the humble Jewish fisherman, lives on in the person of John Paul II, the apostle of all people who continuously brings us the truth. An apostolic pilgrim, he is carrying on the mission of the Master, of the Good Shepherd. He reaches to every corner of the world, and to those who cannot come to Rome, he reaches out to the poor, and indirectly he kindles a desire to visit St. Peter's. The number of pilgrims is constantly rising.

With this book, that is simple yet profound, easy to read, cultural and spiritual at once, Father Giuliani offers a guide that could be copied by every sanctuary, or rather every church in the world. No matter how small a church may be, whether it is grand or simple, ancient or modern, it has a history of its own that is always interesting. And that history should always be set out, in a book or even just a leaflet. With a text such as this written by Father Giuliani, every guide becomes a missionary. Even professional guides can become spiritual guides in the broad sense, helping to show way towards peace and brotherhood for people of all faiths and creeds.

† Emmanuele Clarizio
Titular Archbishop of Anzio
President of the Peregrinatio ad Petri Sedem

Plan of
St. Peter's Basilica

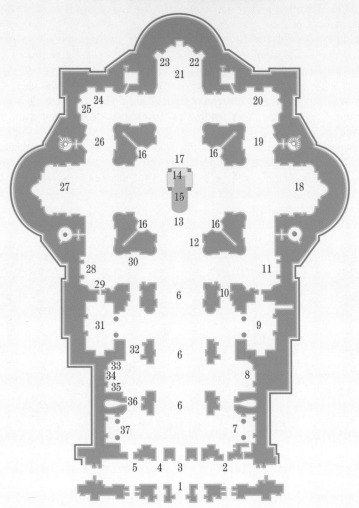

1. Portico or Atrium
2. Holy Door
3. Center Door
4. Door of Good and Evil
5. Door of Death
6. Interior
7. Pietà by Michelangelo
8. Monument to Pius XII
9. Chapel of the Blessed Sacrament
10. Monument to Gregory XIII
11. Gregorian Chapel
12. Statue of St. Peter
13. Baldachin by Bernini
14. Altar of the Confession
15. Tomb of St. Peter
16. The four Relics
17. The Dome
18. The Right Transept
19. Monument to Pope Clement XIII
20. Chapel of St. Petronilla
21. Chapel of the Cathedra
22. Monument to Pope Urban VIII
23. Monument to Pope Paul III
24. Chapel of St. Leo the Great
25. Madonna of the Column
26. Monument to Pope Alexander VII
27. Left Transept
28. Chapel of St. Gregory the Great
29. Monument to Pope Pius VII
30. Chapel of the Transfiguration
31. Choir Chapel
32. Monument to Pope Innocent VIII
33. Monument to Pope John XXIII
34. Chapel of St. Pius X
35. Monument to Pope Benedict XV
36. Stuart Monument
37. Baptistry Chapel

Introduction

This book is for you, be you pilgrim or tourist, who have perhaps long wanted to come to the Eternal City. Perhaps you have wanted to enter the embrace of Bernini's colonnade and listen to the message of these ancient stones, the foundation stones of St. Peter's.

Here, amidst the colorful crowds, you will feel the emotional impact of the enormous basilica, the "Cathedral of Humanity". And, you will immediately see that all people are welcome.

People have been coming here for centuries; pilgrims have come to the tomb of St. Peter to pray for enlightenment, strength and courage. We hope this booklet will help you become acquainted with and understand the treasures of art and faith that are here. They were created by the Western world's greatest artists and with a dual purpose, to be admired and to convey a profound spiritual message.

Look through the book slowly; you will find "new friends" whose faith may give you new courage. Look around, listen. You will hear a message of faith and suffering, of battles won or apparently lost. But mainly you will feel a Presence; the presence of the Lord who has guided Christians of old and Christians today, and who is still reaching out to guide us all.

Please accept our invitation, to continue on this wonderful journey through the history of the faith. Many others took their first steps, right here in St. Peter's Basilica   (G.G.)

Plan of Nero's Circus and the Two Basilicas

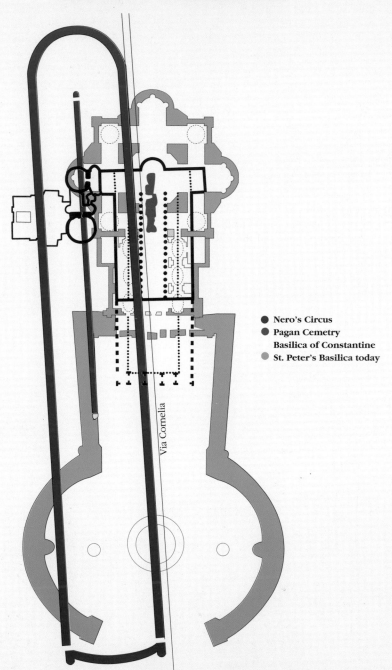

- ● Nero's Circus
- ● Pagan Cemetery
- Basilica of Constantine
- ● St. Peter's Basilica today

Via Cornelia

The largest and perhaps most impressive basilica in the world rises over the pagan cemetery that extended from the Via Cornelia, the road that connected the Tiber to the Via Aurelia, and flanked Nero's Circus. It was exactly here, that around 67 A.D., during the first persecution of Christians launched by Nero that the Apostle Peter was crucified during a spectacle that included battles between slaves, gladiators and wild beasts. The Christians immediately took Peter's body and buried it in the cemetery near the Circus. The remains of that cemetery can still be seen today beneath the basilica. Excavations between 1939 and 1950 unearthed both the tomb and the relics of the apostle.

Pope Anacletus (76-88), Peter's immediate successor, built a small chapel over the Apostle's tomb. It immediately became a place of worship and pilgrimage for the early Christians, later popes and those who came to Rome in spite of the risks of the ferocious persecutions, so that could pray at the tomb of the Prince of the Apostles.

The persecutions came to an end under Constantine, the emperor who had a vision of the Cross as a sign of victory. Under his reign the church's spiritual leadership was officially recognized with the famous Edict of Milan in 313. It was Constantine who, in 324, built a lavish basilica over the entire cemetery and part of the circus. The main altar was to stand over Peter's simple tomb. Legend tells us that the emperor removed his rich robes and began digging the foundations with his own hands. He personally filled and carried away twelve baskets of earth: one for each apostle.

The circus had to be destroyed to build the church (much of the circus structures were made of wood) and many tombs had to be removed and reburied. According to Roman law, only the the Emperor, the supreme authority, could give permission to tamper with grave sites. Then, to position the main altar over St. Peter's tomb, half the hillside sloping down towards the circus had to be excavated. The cuts in the hill are still visible to this day on the northern side, outside the Basilica.

The old, five-aisled basilica was 118 meters long, 64 meters wide and had 88 columns,

Nero's Circus

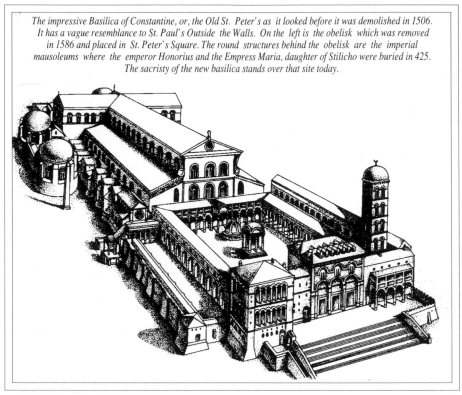

The impressive Basilica of Constantine, or, the Old St. Peter's as it looked before it was demolished in 1506. It has a vague resemblance to St. Paul's Outside the Walls. On the left is the obelisk which was removed in 1586 and placed in St. Peter's Square. The round structures behind the obelisk are the imperial mausoleums where the emperor Honorius and the Empress Maria, daughter of Stilicho were buried in 425. The sacristy of the new basilica stands over that site today.

Basilica of Constantine, or the Old St. Peter's Basilica

that is, 22 in each row. It was begun in 324; the main portion was finished in just five years, and was consecrated by Pope St. Sylvester (314-335). Over the following decades it was embellished with a portico, that soon became a preferred burial place for popes, kings and emperors who wanted their final resting places near that of St. Peter. During previous centuries many simple faithful had been buried there, giving further proof of the authenticity of the legend that this is, indeed, the site of St. Peter's tomb. Later, a bell-tower, with 12 windows on each of its six storeys was built, as was a double-portico that was used for papal blessings. The basilica had 120 altars, 27 of which were, in some way, dedicated to the Virgin Mary. Of the 700 oil lamps, 120 burned around St. Peter's tomb. The basilica was a focal point of spiritual

life: Peter and other early Christians were martyred on the site, and Peter was buried there. Peter's successors chose the site as their seat, and it was there that relics from the Holy Land such as the relic of the Holy Cross, St. Veronica's veil and the lance that had pierced the side of Christ were kept. The interior of the basilica was resplendent with rare marble, mosaics of all colors, shining metals, draperies, tapestries and precious stones. The floor around the tomb of St. Peter was covered with gold and silver. These priceless treasures were stolen when the shrine was sacked by the Visigoths (410), the Vandals (455), the Saracens (846), the Normans (1084) and others who, attracted by their material value, totally ignored their spiritual significance. In fact, the countless pilgrims who travelled to Rome from all over the world were not interested in gold or silver, they only cared about *"videre Petrum"*, seeing the shrine, strengthening their faith and enriching their spirit. In order to help this constant flow of pilgrims, the *Scholae Peregrinorum* sprang up around the old basilica; providing hostels and hospices for pilgrims of all nations: Frisians, Franks, Czechs, Teutons, Flemish, Hungarians, Illyrians, Saxons, Lombards, Armenians, and Abyssians, they came from Corsica and from north of the Po River and every other part of the world. Rome was becoming the *patria communis*. The opportunity to live, eat and sleep so close to the tomb of St. Peter, gatekeeper of heaven, for even a short time was considered a step towards salvation. This international "facility" had to close down when work was begun on the new basilica. The only *Scholae* that remained within the Vatican walls are the Teutonic Church and the Church of St. Stephen of Abyssinia. However, the glorious basilica, where twenty-three emperors had been crowned, that had welcomed pilgrims from every part of the world, that had celebrated the first Holy Year (1300), described by Dante and immortalized by Giotto's paintings, that had confirmed and strengthened Christian faith, began to show the ravages of time after twelve centuries. In the XVI century, after several attempts at restorations, the Basilica with its enormous history and traditions, was at risk. Reluctantly, the decision was made to demolish it, but on the brighter side, another decision was made, to erect an even greater one, the basilica as it exists today, on the same site.

In 1506 Pope Julius II laid the first stone of the new basilica and started construction that was to last for onehundred and twenty years. The greatest artists of the era worked on it. Bramante (1444-1514), Raphael (1483-1520), Michelangelo (1475-1564), Fontana (1541-1607), Della Porta (1540-1602), Bernini (1598-1680), Maderno (1559-1629) and others. Faith and genius paid homage to Peter's tomb and the new basilica, with its enormous dome reaching skyward, continues its hymn of praise to the greatness of God and the honor of St. Peter.

St. Peter's Basilica today

«I am the good shepherd...And other sheep I have which are not of this fold: them also I must bring...and there shall beone fold and one shepherd» (John, 10: 14-16).

B ernini (1598-1680) built his colonnade between 1656 and 1667. Its magnificent design symbolizes the Church, two arms embracing all humanity, "Catholics, to confirm their faith, and others to welcome them to the Church and show them the Way."

It is 340 meters wide, with a 240 meter central ellipse enclosed by four rows comprising 284 columns with 88 pillars. The balustrade is topped by 140 statues of saints, while below, at the foot of the grand staircase, the two 8-meter high statues of Saints Peter and Paul seem to welcome the pilgrims to the basilica.

In the center of the square stands the obelisk which the Emperor Caligula had brought to Rome from Egypt to decorate Nero's Circus. In 1586, by order of Pope Sixtus V, the obelisk was moved to where it stands now, to embellish the square, and mainly so that all pilgrims who come here can see this silent witness of St. Peter's martyrdom. Over 900 workers, 140 horses and 47 winches were needed to raise the obelisk. The entire project was designed and supervised by the architect Domenico Fontana (1543-1607).

The obelisk is 25 meters high, 41 if we

count the base and the cross on top. It is also a sun dial, its shadows marks noon over the signs of the zodiac in the white marble disks in the paving of the square. Two lavish fountains designed by Carlo Maderno (1559-1629) and Carlo Fontana (1634-1714) symbolize the purification needed to enter the house of the Lord. During Conclaves, the square is filled with faithful, waiting for the white smoke from the chimney of the Sistine Chapel to announce the election of a new pope, who then comes out on the balcony of the Basilica to give his blessing to Rome and the world (Urbi et Orbi). From April to October every year the square is filled with pilgrims from all over the world for the general audience on Wednesdays and the major religious celebrations (Palm Sunday, Easter, Beatifications, etc.).

Every Sunday, at noon, the faithful gather in the square to recite the Angelus and receive the Pope's blessing when he comes to his window (the next to the last one on the top floor, on the right).

In addition to being the most beautiful square in the world, it is the most peaceful and most cosmopolitan.

The Dome

The impressive dome which soars majestically towards the sky (h.137 meters) was designed by Michelangelo (1475-1564). It looks like a giant tiara, crowning the tomb of St. Peter. Construction, ordered by Pope Sixtus V was begun in 1588 and took only 22 months. Eight-hundred men worked day and night (by torchlight) under the direction of the architect Giacomo Della Porta (1540-1602) who increased the overall height by seven meters and modified Michelangelo's

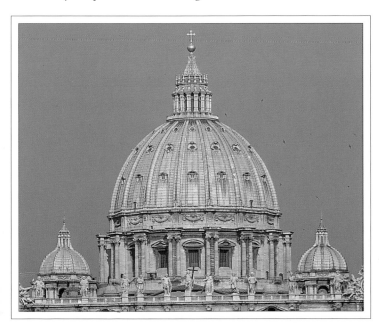

«Dome of St. Peter's...you are both an offering of man's to God and a symbol of the fold which has no limits in its capacity to receive, which turns no one away and which shelters all men from God's wrath and from the temptations of evil.» (Arturo C. Jemolo)

«Thine, O Lord, is the greatness, and the power, and the glory, and the victory, and the majesty: for all that is in the heaven and in the earth is thine.» (1 Chr. 29:11).

original plans. It is the largest dome ever built at that height. "The immense structure seems to be balanced against the Roman sky, as if by miracle, free of all weight. It is awesome, and yet its lines are simple. This rare blend of strength and grace, of power and faith seems to summarize the genius of Michelangelo himself and it has become the monumental symbol of the Rome of Christ and the Popes much as the Colosseum is the symbol of the Rome of the Cesars" (Carlo G. Paluzzi). It can be seen from anywhere in Rome and Catholic pilgrims salute it solemnly as soon as they glimpse it from afar, because it is the symbol of the Church and the seat of the Papacy. It is almost impossible to imagine the Roman skyline without its grandiose outlines which are a source of joy and spiritual comfort. Even the sun caresses it with its rays so that it has been described as "red at dawn, opaline in the early morning, silver in the afternoon and purple at twilight." (G. Turcio).

The Façade

The impressive, 45 meter high and 114 meter long travertine façade was designed by Carlo Maderno. It is crowned by thirteen, six-meter high statues; in the center is the Redeemer blessing the pilgrims who come from all over the world. He is flanked by St. John the Baptist and eleven Apostles, because the statue of St. Peter, with that of St. Paul is located on the staircase below.

The eight giant columns are 27 meters tall and nearly three meters in diameter. They support the cornice along which are the words dedicating the basilica to Peter, Prince of the Apostles, by Pope Paul V (1605-1621).

In the center of the façade is the balcony from which the election of the new pope is announced. The words are part of Western history *"Nuntio vobis gaudium magnum! Habemus Papam"*. The newly elected pope stands on that same balcony to give his first blessing *Urbi et Orbi*, while the members of the College of Cardinals, stand on the balconies on either side. It is from the same balcony that on Easter and Christmas, the Pope gives his blessing. Beneath the balcony there is a fine marble bas-relief sculpture of Jesus handing the keys to Peter.

To the left, below the large clock is the famous bell of St. Peter's, it weighs 10,000 kgs and is 3 and a half meters in diameter. Five, elegant wrought iron gates, flanked by marble columns lead into the atrium of the Basilica.

The terrace above affords an unforgettable view of the fine geometry of St. Peter's square, and the domes, churches, *palazzi*, parks and pines of Rome.

A flight of twenty-five steps lead to the basilica's entrance, and easily brings to mind the jubilant song of the pilgrims as they reached the Temple in Jerusalem: "I was glad when they said unto me: 'Let us go into the house of the Lord'. Our feet shall stand within thy gates, O Jerusalem. Whither the tribes go up, the tribes of the Lord, ...to give thanks unto the name of the Lord...Pray for the peace of Jerusalem: they shall prosper that love thee. Peace be within thy walls, and prosperity within thy palaces. For my brethren and companions' sakes, I will now say, Peace be within thee. Because of the house of the Lord our God, I will seek thy good." (Ps.121: 1-2, 4, 6-9).

The Portico or Atrium

T he solemn, luminous portico, richly decorated with stucco and medallions depicting scenes from the construction of the Old Saint Peter's Basilica, with statues of the first thirty-two martyred popes is so noble and

«For a day in thy courts is better than a thousand. I had rather be a doorkeeper in the house of my God than to dwell in the tents of wickedness.» (Ps. 83:11).

majestic as to seem like a basilica itself. It was designed by Maderno in 1612, with elegance and grace. It is 71 meters long, 13 meters wide and 20 high. Its five monumental bronze doors take the faithful into the basilica. Pilgrims respectfully stop in front of the Holy Door, which is somewhat smaller and is opened only once every 25 years.

In the middle of fine marble floor is the coat of arms of Pope John XXIII who convened the second ecumenical Vatican Council. The more than three thousand bishops who attended this historic meeting on 11 October 1962 entered the basilica this way. To the left and right of the Door of Death there are two ancient plaques affixed to the wall. The first commemorates the donation by Pope Gregory II (715-731) of fifty-six olive trees at Anagni near Rome to provide oil for the lamps that continually burn in front of St. Peter's tomb. The second bears the elegy that Charlemagne composed on the death of Pope Adrian I in 795.

A third plaque is located on the wall to the left of the Holy Door, it is engraved with part of the Bull by which Pope Boniface VIII declared the first Holy Year in 1300. In the lunette above the central door is Giotto's famous mosaic "La Navicella" that he made for that first Holy Year in the old basilica. The many marble columns that grace the portico come from the old basilica. At the right end of the portico is Bernini's statue of the Emperor Constantine when he had the vision of the cross with the words "In this sign, conquer." Facing it is the statue of Charlemagne, the first Holy Roman Emperor who was crowned in St. Peter's by Pope Leo III on Christmas night in 799.

The Holy Door

This door is usually opened every twenty-five years during the Holy Year. It was also opened recently for the Jubilee years in 1933-34 and 1983-84. The Holy Door represents Christ, the Savior, Shepherd and Teacher. He said of himself, "I am the door: by me if any man enters in he shall be saved." (John, 10:9).

This bronze door, made by the artist Vico Consorti (1950) is decorated with scenes on the subject of sin and forgiveness focused on the Gospel parables of mercy.

1. *When Adam and Eve were banished from the Garden of Eden, it seemed that a door was closed forever, but the Annunciation opened the door of life through forgiveness brought by Redemption.*

2. *The Lord is waiting for us at the Holy Door to a) restore joy to those who have wasted the gift of baptism; b) to look for the lamb lost amidst the evils of the world; c) to await the return of the prodigal son; d) to*

«I will arise and go to my father, and will say unto him, Father, I have sinned against heaven and before thee.»(Luke, 15:18).

heal those who are maimed by sin.
3. *Much has been forgiven in exchange for much love"* a) *Love and forgiveness;* b-c) (St. Peter is the key figure) are the elements needed to find the Lord who, crucified by sin, spoke the words, "Today, you will be with me in Paradise".
4. *Lack of faith, a) pride and b) sin that prevent the development of faith will be eliminated by Jesus who said "Forgive us our* sins" b) the Lord is waiting for us at that other door, which is our heart, where he knocks every day because he wants to enter "Sto ad ostium et pulso" (I stand at the door and knock); d) To the left of the Holy Door is the Door of the Sacraments designed by Venanzo Crocetti (1950). The imagery on this door is easy to understand because it lists the sources of Grace, which are the seven sacraments.

Center Door

This is truly an historical door, as it was part of the old basilica. It was made by the Florentine artist Antonio Averulino known as Filarete (1400-1469) in the year 1455.

The rich and elegant workmanship is a hymn to Christ, the Virgin Mary and to the apostles Peter and Paul. At the top are the Savior enthroned, giving a blessing, and the Virgin Mary, humble and reverent. This was one of the most widely used themes in the Middle Ages: the Church as a family. Where there is the Father, there must also be the Mother, otherwise it would be cold and heartless.

In the center, are the impressive, standing figures of Peter and Paul, the two great pillars of the Roman

«They shall persecute you, delivering you up to the synagogues, and into prisons, being brought before kings and rulers for my name's sake. Settle it therefore in your hearts, not to meditate before what ye shall answer: For I will give you a mouth and wisdom, which all your adversaries shall not be able to gainsay nor resist.» (Luke 21: 12, 14-15).

blade, the word of God. At his feet is an elegant vase of flowers. Peter is the keeper of the keys. He is depicted as holding the Gospel in one hand and giving the keys over to the kneeling Pope Eugenius IV who had commissioned this door.

The last two panels show the Apostles condemned to death by Nero seated on his throne. Peter is being forcibly led to the Vatican hill where he would be crucified upside down. Paul, on the other hand was a Roman citizen, and met a less cruel death. He was made to kneel, he was blindfolded and he was beheaded with a single stroke of a sword. We see Paul, in the middle of the same panel as he emerges from a cloud to return the

Church. Paul holds a sword, symbol not only of his martyrdom, but of that double-edged veil to Plautilla: the girl had given it to him to cover his eyes before he was executed.

The DOOR of Good and Evil

This door was presented to Pope Paul VI (1963-1978) in honor of his eightieth birthday on 2 September 1977. It was designed and cast in bronze by the artist Luciano Minguzzi. It develops the theme of the ancient conflict between Good and Evil.

The figures on the right leaf portray Good. a) Saint Augustine who fought the Manichean heresy during his life is shown closing a heretic's mouth because truth must triumph and error must be repudiated; b) Good is symbolized by the two doves building a nest, because love is creative; c) the gift of Baptism is great, it purifies and makes us true children of God. One of the fruits of good is to be free of excess patriotrism and racial discrimination. A kneeling, weaponless soldier receives Communion from a Black cardinal; *d) Vatican II tried to unite humanity in a single, big family. Pope John XXIII and Pope Paul VI are shown with the three cardinals who presided over the committees. e) Knowing that*

«For a good tree bringeth not forth corrupt fruit; neither doth a corrupt tree bring forth good fruit. A good man out of the good treasure of his heart bringeth forth that which is good, and an evil man out of the evil treasure of his heart bringeth forth that which is evil.» (Luke 6, 43-45).

one is free of earthly bonds, like Lazarus who rose from the dead and was released from his death clothes, and having a good friend as the Archangel Raphael was a friend to Tobias, are all positive consequences for those who seek the Good.

The left leaf portrays Evil: a) Saints Vitalis and Agricola master and slave were crucified on the same cross because they were Christians b) the owl is the symbol of evil because it stalks the dove, symbol of Good; c) the martyrdom of Saint Andrew, Peter's brother, together with the ferocity of slavery, is one of the poisonous fruits of evil that brings dishonor upon the dignity of man who was created in the image of God; d) murder only comes from the evil one; man, the slave of evil tortures his brothers for religious or political reasons; *e) Cain, who killed his brother, Abel, is both victim and slave of evil, like the thief who did not even convert when Christ died and a crow picks at his brain.*

The Door of Death

In the past funeral processions left the basilica through this door, so it was originally known as the Door of Judgement. It was ordered by Pope John XXIII (1959-1963) who commissioned the sculptor Giacomo Manzù to create this modern bronze masterpiece. He brilliantly developed the theme of Death that leads to holiness.

1) The death of two of the greatest fig-

ures who ever had human form: Christ as he is being taken down from the cross, and the Virgin Mary, just dead, rapidly ascending to heaven so that her pure body not be corrupted by the tomb;

2) this high relief, a sign of Christian hope, depicts the cut vine and stalks of wheat: their "deaths" give us bread and wine, symbols of the Eucharist and antidotes of death, because "he who eats of this bread will have eternal life".

3) this panel is filled with solemn drama: a) the violent death of an innocent (Abel) and the serene death of the just (St. Joseph); b) the awful death of the first pope, (St. Peter) and the

«Therefore, be ye also ready: for in such an hour as ye think not the Son of man cometh.» (Matt. 24:44).

holy death at prayer (John XXIII); c) the cruel death of the first martyr (St. Stephen) and the bitter death of Pope Gregory VII in exile; d) agonizing death in space and the sorrowful death of the mother who outlives her child.

4) even the six animals below the last panels recall the drama of death, with an admonition to remain faithful.

5) On the inner part of the door, in addition to the artist's handprint, there are two scenes that refer to the second Vatican council. The door handles themselves recall the theme of death: they are shaped like handkerchiefs, used to wipe away tears of sorrow.

The Interior

O nce inside the basilica the visitor immediately becomes aware that this is not only the shrine containing St. Peter's tomb, it is also a holy place of the religion for which Peter so generously gave his life. Here Catholics come to profess their faith in God, in Jesus Christ and in their Church, which is "one, holy, catholic and apostolic," and to reaffirm their promise to remain faithful to Peter in the person of his successors. "Here we are in St. Peter's, in the Vatican Basilica, the most beautiful church of the most beautiful religion in the world...How can one but adore a religion that is capable of producing such beauty?" (Stendhal).

A brief stop at the beginning of the central nave offers a magnificent view: grandeur, splendor, spiritual peace and serene joy come together here. The immensity of the place, the harmonious ceiling, the colored marble floors, the statues of the saints who founded religious orders and congregations in the niches of the pillars, in fact, they are the jewels and true pillars of the Church. In the middle, as if to mark the holiest place, the tomb of St. Peter, stands the magnificent baldachin designed by Bernini beneath Michelangelo's majestic dome.

Along the perimeter of the central nave, of the transept, and above the arches, por-

trayed as female figures are the twenty-eight Christian and human virtues that help us as we travel on our journey towards God, source of all that is good.

The basilica extends over an area of 25,616 square meters; the outside perimeter is 1,778 meters long. It has 44 altars, 11 domes, 778 columns, 395 statues and 135 mosaic pictures. The central nave is 187 meters long, 140 meters wide at the transept, 46 meters high. The dome rises 137 meters into the Roman sky.

This building, the creation of some of the world's greatest artists, is a lasting testimony of faith in the Church. It embodies the majesty, power, glory, strength and beauty of God who welcomes all to His church.

Before taking a look at the most important artworks inside the basilica, let us stop a moment. Two pairs of chubby little angels support the holy water stoups, and they remind us to respect the silence of this place of worship because, "My house shall be called of all nations the house of prayer" (Mark 11:17).

The Pietà by Michaelangelo

T his is probably the world's most famous sculpture of a religious subject. Michelangelo carved it when he was 24 years old, and it is the only one he ever signed. The beauty of its lines and expression leaves a lasting impression on everyone.

With this magnificent statue Michelangelo has given us a highly spiritual and Christian view of human suffering. Artists before and after Michelangelo always depicted the

Virgin with the dead Christ in her arms as griefstricken, almost on the verge of desperation. Michelangelo, on the other hand, created a highly supernatural feeling.

As she holds Jesus' lifeless body on the her lap, the Virgin's face emanates sweetness, serenity and a majestic acceptance of this immense sorrow, combined with her faith in the Redeemer. It seems almost as if Jesus is about to reawaken from a tranquil sleep and that after so much suffering and thorns, the rose of resurrection is about to bloom.

As we contemplate the Pietà which conveys peace and tranquility, we can feel that the great sufferings of life and its pain can be mitigated.

Here, many Christians recall the price of their redemption and pray in silence. The words may be those of the "Salve Regina" or "Sub tuum presidium" or another prayer.

After Peter's Tomb, the Pietà Chapel is the most frequently visited and silent place in the entire basilica.

It is said that Michelangelo had been criticized for having portrayed the Virgin Mary as too young since she actually must have been around 45-50 years old when Jesus died. He answered that he did so deliberately because the effects of time could not mar the virginal features of this, the most blessed of women. He also said that he was thinking of his own mother's face, he was only five when she died: the mother's face is a symbol of eternal youth.

«From this land where pilgrims go, comforted by their faith in the resurrection, we look to you, our sweetness, our hope, lead us with your voice, to show us someday, after our exile, Jesus, the blessed fruit of your womb. O clement, o holy, o sweet Virgin Mary» (Prayer of Pope Pius XII).

Monument to Pope Pius XII

Pope Pius XII (1939-58), who guided the Church during the difficult days of World War II could not fail to be honored in the Basilica he loved so dearly.

The *Cardinales ab eo creati* ordered a monument to him that was made by the famous artist Francesco Messina in 1964.

A high pedestal further augments the already tall figure of the pope who stands majestically in the robes of his authoritiy and spiritual power. His farreaching gaze extends to the horizon and imminent war. With his famous gesture, hand raised in blessing, he symbolically tries to stop the oncoming disaster.

His prophetic words to the heads of state before the outbreak of the war have become famous "Nothing is lost with peace, everything can be lost with war."

Opposite this monument is the one to his predecessor Pope Pius XI (1922-39), the pope of "dauntless faith", of the great social encyclicals, the pope of Catholic Action, of the missions, of the Eucharistic Congresses, of the University of the Sacred Heart. This pope, who could foresee the devasting consequences of totalitarian regimes, condemned their doctrines from the beginning. Pius XI was also the first Pope Sovereign of Vatican City, a title recongized by the Lateran Treaty (11 February 1929).

The monument was created by Francesco Nagni (1949).

Under the altar, between the two monuments in a crystal casket are the remains of the Blessed Pope Innocent XI (1676-89). This pope was highly respected for having encouraged morality in public life and for having contributed to the victory of the Christian forces that defended Vienna against the Turkish siege in 1683.

Above the altar is a mosaic by Pietro Paolo Cristofori (1738), a copy of Domenichino's (1581-1641) Martyrdom of St. Sebastian.

«He that heareth you heareth me; and he that despiseth you despiseth me; and he that despiseth me despiseth him that sent me.» (Luke 10:16).

This is a silent chapel, filled with the scent of flowers and incense. Perhaps it is the most mystical in the entire basilica. The Blessed Sacrament is here for the faithful to see, and it is particularly awe-inspiring for Catholics. It brings to mind the words and melodies of the *Lauda Sion Salvatorem*, the *Pange Lingua* and the *Adoro te devote,* the great hymns written by St. Thomas Aquinas when he composed the Holy Office for the Feast of Corpus Christi.

These hymns seem to develop in a joyous crescendo, following the harmonious lines and colors of the gilded stucco on the ceiling, the gaze of angels in mid-flight, and the slanting rays of light that gently illuminate the space. All this beauty helps the soul, as does the intimacy and silence of this place, the trusting dialogue of prayer which becomes a song of joy.

The tabernacle, by Bernini (1598-1680) is based on the famous Gianicolo temple by Bramante. The two large angels kneeling on the altar watch us, filled with joy and invite us to worship and pray, and to forget the deafening noise of the world for an instant or two. Mesmerized by all this, pilgrims and visitors alike can leave frivolity aside, and contemplate what is really important. The devout may kneel before Christ, their "Bread of Life" who brings the "word of eternal life."

«I am the living bread which came down from heaven: if any man eat of this bread he shall live forever: and the bread that I will give is my flesh, which I will give for the life of this world» (John 6:51).

Monument to Pope Gregory XIII

Before being elected to the papacy, Gregory XIII (1572-1585) taught jurisprudence at the University of Bologna. An expert in law and theology, he was sent by Pope Pius IV to the Council of Trent. As pope he worked hard to support Catholicism when the new Protestant creeds were spreading through Bavaria and Poland. He had direct contacts with many saints: Carlo Borromeo, Filippo Neri, Ignatius Loyola, and Roberto Bellarmino as well as indirect contacts with Saint Theresa d'Avila and Saint John of the Cross. During his papacy Jesuit missions flourished in India, Japan and Brazil; he can also be considered the founder of the Gregorian University; the great master of polyphony, Pierluigi da Palestrina and the poet Torquato Tasso were his protegés. He also issued the Gregorian Calendar. Eminent scientists and astronomers pointed out that the last calendar reform, by Julius Caesar in 45 B.C. contained some errors, and therefore, over the past sixteen hundred years, these errors had grown to 10 days. The correction was made in 1582, October 4th was followed by October 15th. This episode is depicted in the bas-relief carving on the sarcophagus. The pope is shown with famous mathematicians and astronomers including the Jesuit Priest Ignatius Danti, Father Clavius of Bamberg and Antonio Lilio of Calabria, who are well visible because the allegorical figure of Wisdom, with helmet and shield is lifting the drapery to reveal the meeting of scientists presided over by the pope. The figure of the Pontiff may well be the most beautiful in all papal iconograpy. The monument was carved by the Milanese sculptor Camillo Rusconi (1658-1728).

«I am the light of the world: he that followeth me shall not walk in darkness, but shall have the light of life.» (John 8:12).

Gregorian Chapel

In the *Annals* a leaflet much used during the XVI century, it says that this chapel, the first one to be finished according to Michelangelo's designs, is the most beautiful and lavish in the world. It is indeed worthwhile to stop and admire the inlays of colored marble, mother of pearl, and gemstones, the the carved capitals, mosaics of all colors and the enchanting stuccowork on the ceiling.

Above the altar, set into fine marble, is an image of the Virgin Mary.

It was originally in the old basilica and is known as Our Lady of Succour. She joyfully presents Jesus, "blessed fruit of her womb" who will redeem our sins.

After presenting their credentials, to the pope, Catholic diplomats accredited to the Holy See go to the chapel of the Blessed Sacrament in the basilica and stop here to ask the Virgin for her assistance; then they go on to see the Tomb of St. Peter.

In the middle of altar is a porphyry urn containing the remains of St. Gregory of Nazianzus (died 390) who was known as the Luminary of Cappadocia. Together with St. John Chrysostom, Leo the Great and Gregory the Great he was an ardent defender of Church Dogma and a brilliant theologian.

With his colleagues, he now rests in the basilica.

To the right of the chapel is the monument to Pope Gregory XVI (1831-1846), who did much to defend the faith.

«One thing have I desired of the Lord, that will I seek after; that I may dwell in the house of the Lord all the days of my life, to behold the beauty of the Lord and to enquire in his temple.» (Ps.26:4)

Statue of St. Peter

This ancient statue of St. Peter, portrayed as he gives a blessing and preaches, while holding the keys to the kingdom of heaven is famous throughout the world.

Some scholars have attributed it to Arnolfo di Cambio (1245-1302), but others believe that it is a V century casting.

Pilgrims who come to the Basilica traditionally touch and kiss its foot, so that it is literally worn thin. In the Middle Ages pilgrims who reached Rome, touched and kissed the foot of the statue and prayed to St. Peter asking that he be merciful and open the gates of heaven for the them if they died during the pilgrimage.

On 29 June, the feast of St. Peter, the statue is clothed with an amice, alb, tiara, stole, red cope and a ring so that it practically seems to come to life.

Fine marble, Sicilian jasper, green porphyry and the "marble of St. Peter" decorate the pedestal. Behind it, there is what seems to be a fine brocade draping, however, it is actually a mosaic. Above the baldachin, in a circular mosaic is a portrait of Pope Pius IX (1847-1878), the first Pope who in nineteen centuries reigned longer than St. Peter himself, who had led the church for twenty-five years. Pius IX sat on Peter's throne for thirty-one.

The Baldachin by Bernini

This supreme example of Baroque art was the first masterpiece that the twenty-six year old genius, Gianlorenzo Bernini made for St. Peter's Basilica. It is impossible not to admire this fantastic, sumptuous bronze canopy supported by four spiral columns, richly decorated with gold, as it majestically rises upward.

It seems to be, and is, a gigantic processional canopy. It is here that pilgrims through the centuries have stopped to pray and honor St. Peter.

Above the four, finely carved white marble pedestals adorned with the three bees of the Barberini family crest (Pope Urban VIII, 1623-1644 who commissioned the canopy was a Barberini) rise the spiralling columns.

They are decorated with gold olive and laurel branches, and graceful little putti. The first part of the columns with helicoidal fluting, typical of Roman tombs symbolizes the soul as it moves heavenward.

Above the columns, weighing a total of

37,000 kgs, is the impressive draping, decorated with festoons that seem to flutter in the breeze.

The white dove in the middle symbolizes the Holy Spirit, and above the capitals, four angels hold wreaths of flowers, while other smaller ones hold the symbols of the papacy: tiara, keys, sword and the Gospel. Above it all is a cross set on a globe, at a height of 29 meters.

It is well known that in creating these columns with their ascending curves, Bernini drew on ancient models. Some sources say that the vine-leaf decorated columns from the old Basilica came from ancient Greece, others say they were from Solomon's Temple in Jerusalem. These eight columns (plus one which is in the Vatican treasure) now decorate the loggia of the reliquiaries that Bernini made in the pillars supporting the dove.

This brilliant project was begun in 1624 and was completed after nine years of intensive work. It is the largest known bronze artwork.

"Oh Rome... supreme amongst cities, stained by the red blood of your martyrs...we salute you and bless you..."
(Liturgy)

The altar, reached by climbing seven steps is made of a single block of marble from the Forum of Nerva. Like all altars in early Christian churches, it faces east, and as always, the Pope celebrates Mass facing the people. It is the focal point of the basilica, built over Peter's Tomb, crowned by Bernini's canopy and protected by Michelangelo's dome.

It is the third altar built over Peter's tomb. The first was erected by Pope Gregory the Great (590-604), modifying the one built by Constantine; the second was built by Pope Calixtus (1119-1124), and this, the third one, was built by Pope Clement VIII (1592-1605). It is known as the Main or Papal Altar because it is here that the Pope presides over religious ceremonies, its real name, however, is the altar of the confession, in the sense of a confession of faith. Peter is buried beneath it; by professing his belief and faith in Christ, Peter accepted martyrdom. And it is here that generations of Christians have been coming to profess their faith and the twelve articles of the Apostolic Creed:

¹ I believe in God the Father Almighty, Creator of heaven and earth; and in Jesus Christ, His only Son, our Lord;

² Who was conceived by the Holy Ghost, born of the Virgin Mary, suffered under Pontius Pilate, was crucified, died and buried. He descended into Hell;

³ The third day He arose again from the dead;

⁴ He ascended into heaven, sitteth at the right hand of God, the Father Almighty;

⁵ Thence He shall come to judge the living and the dead.

⁶ I believe in the Holy Ghost, the Holy Catholic Church, the communion of saints, the forgiveness of sins, the resurrection of the body, and life everlasting. Amen".

«Therefore, if thou bring thy gift to the altar, and there remem-berest that thy brother hath ought against thee; Leave there thy gift before the altar, and go thy way; first be reconciled to thy brother, and then come and offer thy gift.» (Matt. 5:23-24).

This is the heart and holiest place in the basilica. It was and is the goal of countless pilgrims who come to Rome from all over the world to *videre Petrum. Petrus est hic.* Peter is here, for two thousand years, in a humble, simple tomb over which the magnificent triumphal basilica was built. It seems that Jesus' words have a material value as well: "You are Peter and upon this rock I will build my church." Here we are in the spiritual and physical center of Christianity. From the tomb of St. Peter, the Gospel spread throughout Europe and then to the whole world. After the Holy Sepulchre from which Jesus rose, this is the most venerated tomb in the world. In the year 195 Gaius wrote, "Go to the Vatican on the Via Ostia and there you will find the trophies, (the tombs) of the founders of this Church." In the sacellum above Peter's tomb in a richly decorated niche is a fine silver casket containing the Palls, white wool stoles embroidered with six black crosses that the pope gives to the patriarch and metropolian as a constant reminder to be faithful to Christ and to Peter. Day and night, 99 oil lamps burn along the railing that circles the shrine and along the two semicircular ramps. They are symbols of faith, love, prayer for Christians. Here, the faithful

Once again we hear his words: «Ye also, as lively stones, are built up a spiritual house, an holy priesthood, to offer up spiritual sacrifices acceptable to God by Jesus Christ. But ye are a chosen generation, a royal priesthood, an holy nation, a peculiar people; that ye should show forth the praises of him who hath called you out of darkness into his marvelous light; Which in time past were not a people, but are now the people of God: which had not obtained mercy but now have obtained mcercy. Dearly beloved, I beseech you as strangers and pilgrims, abstain from fleshly lusts, which war against the soul. Having your conversation honest among the Gentiles that whereas they speak against you as evildoers, they may by your good works, which they shall behold, glorify God.» (1 Pet. 2:5,9-12).

humbly profess their faith, repeating the words taught by Peter, the Lord's Prayer and the Creed.

There are four niches, approximately 10 meters high in the base of the pillars that support the dome. Each niche contains a statue: St. Veronica, St. Helena, St. Longinus and St. Andrew, they are the works of F. Mochi, A. Bolgi, G.L. Bernini and F.Duquesnoy, respectively. The chapels above the niches were created to contain the relics of these saints. They were designed and built by Bernini, and are decorated with rare marble, ancient columns and figures of praying angels.

Saint Veronica, *was the poor pious woman whom Jesus cured, and who met him again on the Calvary where she wiped his face when he fell under the weight of the Cross. Miraculously, he left the image of his face on the cloth. The crusaders brought a "veil of Veronica" to Rome from Jerusalem. It was highly venerated, especially during the Middle Ages and was mentioned by Dante in the Divine Comedy (Paradise, XXXI, 104) and in the Vita Nuova (40,1).*

St. Helena *was the mother of the Emperor Constantine. Near the Calvary in Jerusalem she found part of the True Cross. This precious relic was brought to Rome*

F. Mochi - St. Veronica   A. Bolgi - St. Helena

and for centuries was venerated in the Church of the Santa Croce in Gerusalemme of Rome that had been built by St. Helena. Since 1629 this relic is in St. Peter's, in a gold, cross-shaped case.

St. Longinus was the attendant of the Roman centurion who had to ascertain that Jesus was dead. He pierced his side with a lance from which "blood and water" flowed. Longinus became a Christian along with the centurion who declared Christ to be the Son of God (Matt. 27,54). The lance was given to the crusaders, but was stolen by the Saracens. It was brought to Rome as a gift of the Sultan Bayazet, son of Mohammed II, in 1492.

St. Andrew Apostle was St. Peter's brother. He evangelized Greece where he was crucified on the cross that still bears his name. In 1400 Greek Christians sent his skull to Rome so that it would rest near his brother, Peter. In 1966 Pope Paul VI sent this precious relic as an ecumenical gift to the church of St. Andrew of Patraxos.

The three relics of the Passion are now in the chapel above the statue of St. Veronica. During Holy Week they are shown to the faithful who are blessed with them.

«We adore you O Christ, and bless you, because you have redeemed the world with your Holy Cross.» (Liturgy).

G.L. Bernini - St. Longinus

F. Duquesnoy - St. Andrew

— 29 —

After the tomb of Peter, we raise our eyes to admire his glory.

The splendor of the 96 figures in the mosaic is overwhelming, the gaze is drawn towards the center, to the high lantern that rises another 18 meters where, as if in a vision, is the glorious figure of the Eternal Father, with arms outstretched in blessing towards Peter's tomb. He seems to be repeating Jesus' words to Peter, "Blessed are you, Simon, son of Jona". We can read the words of Peter's investiture that circle the dome "Thou art Peter, and upon this rock I will build my church. And I will give unto thee the keys of the kingdom of heaven." (Matt. 16, 18-19).

The dome is decorated in mosaic in the three colors of Medieval mysticism, blue, gold and red. The triumphal decoration is divided into sixteen sections that converge at the top of the dome and are divided into six horizontal circles:

1. the busts of the first sixteen popes buried in the basilica;

2. the great figure of Christ triumphant surrounded by the Virgin Mary, St. John the Baptist, St. Paul and the Twelve Apostles;

3. sixteen angels holding the symbols and instruments of Christ's passion;

«How excellent is thy loving kindness, O God! Therefore the children of men put their trust under the shadow of thy wings. They shall be abundantly satisfied...and thou shalt make them drink of the river of thy pleasures. For with thee is the fountain of life; in thy light shall we see light.» (Ps. 35, 7-10).

4. flights of winged cherubs;
5. angels reverently looking down at Peter's tomb;
6. flights of winged seraphs.

Standing beneath the dome one gets the impression of belonging not to the "militant" church, but rather to the triumphant church. Although the dome expounds the theory of glory, it also recalls the pain, it rests on pillars in which the relics of Christ's passion are conserved to tell us that only through suffering can we reach God. *Per Crucem ad lucem.*

This triumph was designed by G. Cesari, known as the Cavalier d'Arpino (1568-1640), who completed it in 1603 with the help of the era's best mosaicists, Turchi, Torelli, Rossetti, Abatini and Serafini.

The Right Transept

This big and luminous transept is known as the "Transept of Saints Processus and Martinian" two Roman martyrs who were the warders of St. Peter in the Mamertine prison and whom he converted and baptized.

Their relics are kept in the porphyry urn under the altar. On either side are two columns of antique yellow marble which, along with those of the altar of St. Joseph are believed to be unique.

The mosaic above the altar depicts the cruel martyrdom of the saints, who were killed before their parents' eyes while an angel hands over the palm of martyrdom. The mosaic is a fine reproduction of a painting by the French artist Jean de Boulogne (1640).

On the left of the altar is a mosaic portrayal of the martyrdom of St. Erasmus, the bishop who was killed at Formia during the persecution of Diocletian (303-313).

The altar on the right is dedicated to St. Wenceslas, king and patron saint of Bohemia, martyred because of his Christian faith. The painting by Angelo Caroselli was done in 1740. The ovals on the right and left depict saints Cyril and Methodius, joint patrons of Europe. According to Pope Pius XI they were sons of

«These things have I spoken unto you, that ye should not be offended. They shall put you out of the synagogues: yea, the time cometh, that whosoever killeth you will think that he doeth God service; And these things will they do unto you, because they have not known the Father nor me.» (John 16:1-3)

the Orient, Byzantine by birth, Greek by nationality, Roman by mission, Slav by apostolate and did everything for everyone to achieve the unity of the Catholic church.

The large transept has a history of its own: the sessions of the First Vatican Council were held here from 8 December 1869 to 18 July 1870, and over seven hundred bishops took part. The dogma of papal infallibility was proclaimed here. The council was abruptly interrupted when the Italian troops took Rome on 20 September 1879. It was declared officially concluded ninety years later when, Pope John XXIII convened the Second Vatican Council of over three thousand bishops on 11 October 1962.

Monument to Pope Clement XIII

This splendid monument was carved by Antonio Canova (1757-1822) to honor Pope Clement XIII (1758-1769), his countryman. It was the first neoclassical monument in the Basilica and is one of the most admired.

The extraordinary figure of the Pope is kneeling at the tomb in prayer, in an almost other-worldly state. He was an extremely pious and generous Pope, a gentle man with deep spiritual feelings. He distributed his entire personal fortune to help the poor when famine struck the Latium region in1763-64. With one hand resting on the tomb, the statue personifies Religion holding the Cross, symbol of hope and salvation.

The Hebrew letters on the forehead and belt read: "God is Holy" and "Doctrine and Truth." On the right is the Angel of Death who sadly extinguishes the torch of light.

The two perfectly carved crouching lions seem to take turns guarding the tomb, in fact, one is asleep while the other is fiercely alert.

«Come ye blessed of my Father, inherit the kingdom prepared for you. For I was an hungered and he gave me meat...Inasmuch as ye have done it unto one of the least of these my brethren, ye have done it unto me.» (Matt. 25: 34-35, 40).

The Chapel of Saint Petronilla

According to legend, Saint Petronilla was St. Peter's daughter, she left Jerusalem with him to go to Rome. According to history, Petronilla was a virgin and martyr, from the family of Domitilla. She was Peter's "spiritual daughter" in that he baptized her and showed her the light.

Her body was removed from the catacomb of Domitilla in 750 and was translated to the imperial rotonda in the old basilica, next to the tomb of the empress Mary. The chapel with the tomb of St. Petronilla became that of the kings of France, Pepin and Charlemagne (768). Later, embellished with fine artworks it became the French National Chapel. The French ambassador, Jean Cardinal De Bilhäres commissioned Michelangelo to carve the Pietà for this chapel (1499). Unfortunately, the chapel was demolished when the new basilica was erected (1606). Saint Petronilla's relics are now beneath the altar in the chapel that was consecrated by Pope Paul V in 1623. Notwithstanding the vicissitudes of the centuries, the chapel is still the "French National Chapel". Mass on her feast day, 31 May, is attended by the French community in Rome, including the French ambassador, who venerate the "spiritual sister" of France, the "first daughter of the Church".

Above, the altar is one of the most outstanding mosaics in the basilica, by Pietro Cristofari, first director of the Vatican School of Mosaic, after a painting by Guercino (1590-1666). In a marvelous play of chiaroscuro effects, the mosaic shows the martyrdom and apotheosis of the saint as she is received by Christ.

Saint Petronilla is also depicted in the lunette of the dome, as she is baptized by St. Peter and given Communion by St. Nicodemus.

«Teach me thy way, O Lord; I will walk in thy truth: unite my heart to fear thy name.» (Ps. 85:11).

The Chapel of the Cathedra

This structure is a brilliant creation by Bernini, designed to display the chair on which, according to ancient tradition, St. Peter sat and taught Roman Christians. Pope Alexander VII had the ivory-covered chair put into the gigantic bronze cathedra, with the statues of the Doctors of the Church, St. Ambrose and St. Augustine of the Roman Church and St. Athanasius and St. John Chrysostom of the Greek Church. The religious significance is extremely clear. The Doctors of the Church were always consistent with Peter's teachings as they expounded theological doctrine.

The Gospel does not change because the Holy Spirit, portrayed as a dove flies along the span of the centuries, assisting and accompanying its church. The chair or cathedra of Peter symbolizes the perpetual continuity of the doctrine and its promise of infallibility.

It triumphed over all heresies throughout the centuries.

The fine alabaster window, surrounded by golden clouds and angels flying between rays of light, casts a mystical, warmth through the basilica, especially in the afternoon. It is divided into twelve sections, in homage to the twelve Apostles who carried the words of the Gospel throughout the world.

«One God, one Christ, one Church and one Cathedra...» (St. Cyprian)

Monument to Pope Urban VIII

O n either side of the Chapel of the Cathedra are funerary monuments to two Popes, Urban III and Paul III, patrons of two of the most eminent artists who contributed to the construction of St. Peter's Basilica: Michelangelo and Bernini. Urban VIII (1623-1644) "discovered" the great Neapolitan artist Gianlorenzo Bernini who, with enormous gratitude, dedicated this monument to his patron. The majestic figure of the pope giving a blessing is solemnly dressed in his pontifical robes. Like the monument to Paul III, it is made of bronze, not marble. On either side of the black marble sarcophagus are fine, white marble statues of young women. The first, on the left holding a child in her arms represents Charity who looks sadly at another child pointing at the dead pope. The figure on the left symbolizes Justice who sadly raises her eyes upward to seek comfort from God. In the middle, on the sarcophagus, is a bronze skeleton, Death who holds a scroll with the name of the dead Pope in a bony hand. The three bees of the Barberini family crest are usually

«I am the resurrection and the life: he that believeth in me, though he were dead, yet shall he live. And whosoever liveth and believeth in me shall never die.» (John 11:25-26)

arranged symmetrically, here however, they are facing in different directions, disoriented and confused by the death of their sovereign.

Monument to Pope Paul III

T he name of Pope Paul III (1534-1549) is inexorably linked to the Council of Trent that he convened in 1545.
Paul III was the patron of Michelangelo, whom he convinced to paint the Last Judgement in the Sistine Chapel. The great artist was over seventy when he had completed this monumental masterpiece and the pope ordered him to direct construction of the new St. Peter's Basilica in 1546. It is well known that Michelangelo accept-

«My judge will be he who climbed the tower every day to see if the prodigal son had returned. Is there someone who would not want to be judged by him?» (Auguste Valensin)

ed the assignment and refused any form of payment, because he wanted to work to "render glory to God, honor to St. Peter and for the salvation of his soul." Upon the death of the pope, Michelangelo wrote, "Pope Paul III only showed me kindness." This majestic, impressive monument was sculpted by Guglielmo Della Porta and it shows Michelangelo's influence, especially in the figure of the Pope. Ravaged by age and pain, he is shown blessing the figures of Justice and Prudence. The first is actually a portrait of the pope's sister Julia, famous for her beauty. The second is his mother, Giovannella Gaetani, a strict, dignified old woman who resembled the Cumaean Sybil Michelangelo painted in the Sistine Chapel Originally, this monument which was in the Gregorian Chapel was decorated with two other statues, Peace and Abundance. In 1628 it was moved next to the Chapel of the Cathedra by order of Pope Urban VIII who had commissioned Bernini to build his tomb on the opposite side.

Chapel of Saint Leo the Great

St. Peter's Basilica is honored by containing the tomb and mortal remains of its famous son, the pope St. Leo the Great (440-461), incomparable defender of Church doctrine against heresies. His writings, the Homilies, in classical style are still as current as ever. He was called the "Savior of the West", even though he could not prevent the sack of Rome by the Vandals in 455.

Above the altar where he is buried, there is a majestic, high-relief marble portrait of Leo the Great as he met Attila the Hun, the scourge of god, near Mantua. The Pope's words were convincing, Attila was persuaded not to attack Rome. He told his troops that when the Pope spoke he saw the threatening figures of Peter and Paul with drawn swords before him.

The sculpture was done by Alessandro Algradi (1595-1654) and is the only high relief of this type in the Basilica.

«We are not mute dogs, we are not silent spectators, we are not mercenaries fleeing the world, but we are shepherds who carefully watch over the flocks of Christ. We preach the designs of God to the great and to the small, to the rich and to the poor.» (St. Boniface Bishop)

The Chapel of the Madonna of the Column

A fter the chapel dedicated to St. Leo the Great, beneath the small dome that lets in a soft light to enhance the colored marble in the Basilica, we come to the Chapel of the Virgin of the Column, with an ancient painting of the Virgin on the column that had been part of the Old Basilica. In 1607 the painting, framed by fine marbles and precious alabaster columns was placed on this altar designed by G. Della Porta.

In 1645 the Vatican Chapter ordered golden crowns placed on the head of the Virgin and Infant Jesus. After the second Vatican Council, Pope Paul VI honored her with the title of "Mother of the Church." Then in 1981 Pope John Paul II ordered a mosaic copy placed on the outside wall of the palace overlooking St. Peter's Square when, illuminated during the night, it shines with a graceful smile on those who stop to admire it. The Pope unveiled and blessed it on 8 December of the same year. The light from the dome highlights the altar-frontal which, like many others, was designed by Bernini and reproduced in colored mosaic with such skill that it seems to be an embroidered cloth.

«The Virgin Mary is the summary of the history of the Church and the prophecy of its future. God has given each man, whether he knows it or not, the Virgin Mary, as sister and mother to watch over him and guide his steps through life» (Pope Paul VI).

Monument to Pope Alexander VII

T his monument is Bernini's last masterpiece, done when the artist was eighty years old.

A friend and admirer of Bernini, as soon as he was elected Pope, Alexander VII (1655-1667) asked the great artist to prepare a small coffin for his bedroom because, "I will be a good Pope if I think of death."

During the pontificate of Alexander VII Bernini designed and built the magnificent colonnade in St. Peter's Square, the bronze Cathedra, and the Royal Stair, which along with the Baldachin represents the triumph of Baroque art

in the Vatican. After the death of the pope Bernini, with his still rich imagination, wanted to honor his memory with a great monument that is still admired by thousands every day.

The pope is portrayed kneeling in prayer that is interrupted by the appearance of Death, a gigantic skeleton coming out from under the funeral draping, brandishing an hourglass to show that the time has come. Death is shown with a covered face because it comes to all men, without distinction, even to the Supreme Pontiff.

The monument is crowned by four stat-

ues of the virtues that distinguished the life of Alexander VII, that is Justice, Prudence, Charity and Truth. The last statue which also symbolizes Religion has a sorrowful expression because of the Pope's many vain attempts at resolving the difficult situation that had developed with the Anglican Church. The statue's left foot rests on a globe, and specifically right on England.

The monument is striking because of the different and beautiful types of marble used: the bases are black and white, the colors of mourning, the great funeral drape is made of Sicilian jasper, and the statue of the pope, atop a perfect pyramid is white marble.

Left Transept

The light-filled left transept of the basilica, with its gilded stucco ceiling, is a large chapel that is not open to tourists or the curious. Here there is silence, prayer and devotion. The center altar was dedicated to St. Joseph, Mary's husband, and blessed by Pope John XXIII on 19 March 1963. An ancient sarcophagus on the altar contains the relics of the apostles Simon and Jude Thaddeus.

All the Masses in the Basilica are celebrated here except for Sundays and holy days; Holy Communion is given if requested. The faithful come here to pray, or wait their turn for Confession, the sacrament of reconciliation and peace.

On Good Friday, Pope John Paul II joins the other fathers and hears confessions.

An ancient tradition maintains that this part of the Basilica which rises over what was once Nero's Circus is the exact site of Peter's martyrdom. On the basis of this tradition a fine marble altar was built here, with a mosaic reproduction of Guido Reni's painting of the Crucifixion of St. Peter, head down. The famous composer, Pierluigi da Palestrina (1525-1594) is buried nearby in a lead coffin.

Opposite the altar is a mosaic made to a drawing by Camuccini (1771-1844) portraying St. Thomas, who confused and repentant about having been skeptical, touched Jesus' wounds.

«Those whose sins you forgive, they are forgiven; those whose sins you retain, they are retained» (Jn 20,23).

«God, Father of mercy, who has reconciled the world to himself in the death and resurrection of your Son, and has sent the Holy Spirit for the remission of sins, grant you through the ministry of the Church, forgiveness and peace. And I absolve you from your sins in the name of the Father, the Son, and the Holy Spirit» (Rite of absolution).

Chapel of St. Gregory the Great

In the center of the altar are the mortal remains of Saint Gregory the Great (590-604), one of the greatest pontiffs in the history of the Church. He preferred to be known as the "servant of the servants of God", however the faithful also called him "Consul of God", "Savior of the Church", "Defender of Rome" (he defended the city against the Lombards whom he then converted to Christianity) He evangelized England by sending forty Benedictine

«How beautiful upon the mountains are the feet of him that bringeth good tidings, that publisheth peace; that bringeth good tidings of good, that publisheth salvation.» (Is. 52:7).

monks as missionaries. Gregory's name is also linked to the musical forms he promoted, and even today Gregorian chant resounds with its pure melodies.

In the splendid mosaic above the altar, one of the most perfect in the entire basilica, the saint is depicted as showing the faithful a cloth stained with the blood of martyrs; he encourages them to remain faithful to Christ and to the commitments of Baptism.

To honor this great person, his tomb is surrounded by the four great Doctors of the Church: Saints Ambrose, Augustine, Athanasius and John Chrysostom, in the mosaic on the dome above the altar.

Monument to Pope Pius VII

«Love your enemies, do good to them which hate you; bless them that curse you and pray for them which despitefully use you.» (Luke 6:27-28)

problems inflicted by Napoleon whom the pope himself, for love of peace, consecrated Emperor of France in Notre Dame cathedral in Paris. Later Napoleon took him prisoner and sent him to Fontainebleau. Pius VII, never bore any resentment towards his persecutor and when Napoleon was exiled on the island of St. Helena, the pope made efforts to render the ordeal less bitter. He offered asylum to Napoleon's elderly mother and gave both moral and material assistance to his family.

The dignified effigy of the pope shows fatigue and the signs of his long exile, and yet he is portrayed as blessing both friends and enemies alike.

There is a statue on either side of the monument. Wisdom, crowned with an olive wreath and with an owl, symbol of Christian vigilance, at its feet, acquires knowledge from the Bible. Fortitude is dressed in a lion's skin and treads on a club.

T he successor to Pope Pius VI (1775-1799) who died in exile at Valance, France, victim of Napoleon's power, was the Benedictine monk Barnaba Gregorio Chiaramonti who took the name of Pius VII (1800-1823). His was a difficult pontificate filled with moral and physical These are the two virtues that distinguished the troubled times of this pope's long reign.

The monument was created by the Danish sculptor Thornwaldse and was commissioned by Cardinal Consalvi, loyal secretary of State to Pius VII.

In this chapel it is possible to admire a mosaic reproduction of one of the world's most famous paintings "The Transfiguration" showing Christ on Mount Tabor, Raphael's last painting (1483-1520).
It shows the Lord in a nimbus of bright light, raised in the air with the prophet Elias and Moses, the lawgiver, while the three favored apostles, Peter, James and John gaze on this heavenly scene from earth, wishing that it would last for eternity.
The upper portion of the picture reveals

«Lord, it is good for us to be here: if thou wilt, let us make here three tabernacles; one for thee, and one for Moses, and one for Elias.»(Matt. 17:4).

reveals the tranquil ecstasy, the celestial seren-ity and peace the Lord grants only to those who are with Him and who want to be with Him.

The lower part contrasts strongly with the upper. The figures are agitated, they look at the possessed boy whose father is holding.

All are troubled, and they seem to be seeking a human solution to ills of the spirit. Only an apostle, indicating the Lord on the Mount reminds them, the disheartened and discouraged, of the source of salvation.

In the middle, the kneeling woman symbolizes the Church and its task of bringing peace, hope and faith to the victims of evil. Raphael died young, he was only 37. In his final delirium he asked to see his painting for the last time. His friends brought it to him, and placed it on the bed in which in died on Good Friday, 1520.

The same painting was carried at the the head of the funeral procession to the Pantheon where the great artist is buried and awaits his own transfiguration.

The Choir Chapel

T his is an impressive chapel, with finely carved stalls, and richly decorated with precious marble and gilded stuccowork depicting biblical scenes. It was designed by Giacomo Della Porta and dedicated by Pope Urban VIII in 1627. The canons of the Vatican Chapter meet here on Sundays and holy days to pray and sing the Divine Office. During Holy Years this chapel is the starting point for the procession that goes through the Holy Door to the Cathedra. Even when the chapel is closed by its wrought iron gate, one can see the tomb of one of the greatest defenders of the faith, the great Doctor of the Church St. John Chrysostom, Patriarch of Constantinople (344-407). Above the altar, a mosaic portrays Mary Immaculate with St. Francis of Assisi, St. Anthony of Padua and St. John Chrysostom; the original design was by Perugino.

On 8 December 1854, the date that the Immaculate Conception was solemnly proclaimed, Pope Pius IX placed a gold crown on the Virgin, and 50 years later, a group of noblewomen added a crown of twelve diamond stars.

There is an organ on either side of the chapel and when they are played together, they create magnificent stereophonic effects. Domenico Scarlatti (1695-1728) was the organist of this chapel.

«Praise ye the Lord. Praise God in his sanctuary. Praise Him with the sound of the trumpet, with the harp and organs. Let everything that hath breath praise the Lord.» (Ps. 150)

Monument to Pope Innocent VIII

This is one of the few monuments from the Old Basilica that has survived to this day. Originally it was under the triumphal arch. It was designed by Antonio Pollaiolo (1431-1498) the great bronze sculptor. The Pope (1484-1492) is shown surrounded by the four cardinal Virtues (Prudence, Justice, Fortitude and Temperance) and in the lunette above are the theological Virtues (Faith, Hope and Charity). The pope is seated, and in his left hand holds the spear that pierced Jesus' side, one of the most venerated relics in the basilica. This lance, or spear, jealously guarded by the early Christians was later given to the crusaders so that it could be brought to Rome. It was captured by the Saracens and placed in the religious treasure of Constantinople. Later, it was surprisingly offered to Pope Innocent VIII in 1492 by the Turkish sultan Bayazet, son of Mohammed II under the condition that the Pope would detain the sultan's brother, who was threatening his power. The pope agreed, (as did the brother who was quite happy to stay in Rome) and received the lance.

Beneath the monument the Pope is depicted as laying in serene, peaceful death in a sarcophagus.

It is interesting to note that notwithstanding some corrections made to the black stone at the base of the monument, there is still an error. It reads that America was discovered during the pontificate of Innocent VIII, the fact is that Columbus set sail from Europe eight days after the pope died.

«But one of the soldiers with a spear pierced his side, and forthwith came there out blood and water.» (John 19:34).

Monument to Pope John XXIII

This bronze monument by Emilio Greco is a symbol of the Church's gratitude to the gentle Pope John XXIII (1958-1963) the "Good Pope".

On the upper part angels are coming down to earth to announce the spring of optimism, hope and trust in man. In the center is the impressive, strong and human figure of the Pope visiting prisoners, children and the ill. The expression on his face is not the usual one of joyful optimism, but rather it is preoccupied because of the troubles afflicting today's world.

A young mother holds her child up to the

pope for his blessing. But the child, a symbol of the new generation that rejects the past turns his back on the pope who wants to bless him. On lower left, there is a young seated woman, she is tired, sad and disappointed, perhaps she is supposed to symbolize the politics and philosophies of today that are incapable of solving the difficult problems of a complicated world. At the bottom center, the only figure that looks at the pope with trust is a hungry, scrawny dog, symbolizing humanity that is starving for justice, love and peace. Above, behind the pope is a cardinal who holds his hand over his heart as if to say that the ills of today's world can be solved by listening to the voice of one's own consicence which is the voice of God, everpresent in our hearts.

«When you return home you will see children, caress them and say: "This is the caress of the pope. You may have to dry a tear or two. Say a word of comfort to the suffering. The afflicted should know that the pope is with his children especially in times of trial and bitterness. And finally, let us all remember the bond of charity, and whether singing, or sighing, or crying, be filled with faith in Christ who helps us and hears us, let us proceed on our journey, confident and full of hope.» (John XXIII).

Chapel of Saint Pius X

Before this altar was dedicated to St. Pius X, it was known as the altar of the Presentation of the Virgin Mary in the Temple. She is portrayed as a little girl joyfully going up the steps to the temple with her parents Anne and Joachim. This event is magnificently depicted in mosaic by Romanelli to drawings by the painter Carlo Maratta.

Below the altar, is a crystal coffin containing the body of St. Pius X (1904-1914), *"pauper et dives, mitis et humilis corde"*. The body is dressed in pontifical robes, while the face and hands are covered with silver. The world greatly admired his wisdom and firm government. He helped restore Christian life by issuing wise laws on the religious education of children, youths and adults. His catechism gives clear answers to many religious question He allowed young children to take Communion, promoted the practice of daily communion as a source of virtue and holiness, he reformed the liturgy in the Missal and Breviary as well as sacred music and Gregorian chant. He fought against and condemned modernism which is still the cause of

many evils. He was, however, unable to convince the reigning monarchs and heads of state of his era to avoid the conflict that would shed blood throughout Europe for four long years.
His heart could not stand the vision of so many innocent deaths. He died after having offered his life for peace. On the right pillar he is shown with arms and gaze upraised to heavean. The statue was carved by Pietro Astorgi (1923).

«Blessed are the poor in spirit: for theirs is the kingdom of heaven. Blessed are the meek: for they shall inherit the earth.» (Matt. 5:3,5).

Monument to Pope Benedict XV

T o the left of the Chapel of the Presentation our eyes can admire the monument to the successor of Pius X, Pope Benedict XV (1914-1922) who led the church the difficult years of World War I which he defined as "useless slaughter".

«Peace I leave with you, my peace I give unto you: not as the world giveth.» (John, 14:27).

This pope expended most of his energy and strength in trying to convince the heads of state and governments to put down their arms and meet at a negotiating table to resolve Europe's problems peacefully. He organized charitable institutions to help refugees, deportees, prisoners, the wounded and the persecuted without regard for their political or religious beliefs. Wherever his charity could reach, pain and suffering were diminished. Upon his death, the Turkish Muslims, grateful for his charity and good works, built a monument to him in Istanbul.

In the monument here in St. Peter's, he is portrayed in prayer, kneeling above a tomb that is supposed to symbolize the graves scattered throughout Europe to commemorate the soldiers who fell in battle and the innocent victims of the war. The tomb is delicately decorated with olive branches, symbols of peace. Above the statue is the Virgin Mary, presenting the Infant Jesus, "Prince of Peace" to a world in flames. It was Pope Benedict XV who added the words "Queen of Peace, pray for us" to the Litanies of Loreto. The monument by Pietro Canonica (1869-1959) a renowned sculptor, was unveiled in 1928.

Monument to the Stuarts

This is a stupendous work by the young Antonio Canova; It may seem to be a pagan monument as it recalls the funeral steles of ancient Greece.

However, it is a Christian monument to the last three members of the royal house of Stuart who, because they remained faithful to the Catholic church were removed from the throne of England.

The monument is dedicted to James III (1688-1766) son of James II (1633-1701) the last Stuart to reign over England, Scotland and Ireland, and to his sons Charles Edward (1720-1788) and Henry (1725-1805). Henry, Cardinal Duke of York was the bishop of Frascati (1761) and of Ostia and Velletri as well as archpriest of the Vatican Basilica and Deacon of the Sacred College. After the death of his brother Charles, he took the name of Henry IX and proclaimed himself King of England.

The monument is in line with the underlying tombs in the Vatican Grottoes. The small fronton on top is embellished with a carving of the Stuart coat of arms of two lions rampant. On the lower part, in front of a closed door, symbol of the old and unfortunate dynasty stand two angels whose incomparable beauty blends with their pain. The folded wings and bowed heads express resigned sadness over the mystery of death. All this sadness, however, is dissipated by the comforting words of the bible over the closed door "Happy are those who fall asleep in the Lord." George III, king of England (1738-1820) wanted to forget all monarchical and dynastic rivalry, so he generously financed the cost of this monument.

Opposite the monument to the Stuarts, above the entrance to the dome, is a monument to Maria Clementine Sobieska, the pious niece of the King of Poland, John III and wife to James III Stuart, pretender to the English throne. The woman is portrayed in a mosaic medallion supported by a putto and the personification of Charity.

«Blessed are ye when men shall revile you, and persecute you, and shall say all manner of evil against you falsely, for my sake. Rejoice, and be exceeding glad: for great is your reward in heaven.» (Matt. 5:11-12).

Jesus baptized in the Jordan River by John the Baptist, Peter baptized by Christ, the Centurion baptized by Peter, Peter baptizing his warders, Pope Sylvester baptizing the Emperor Constantine.

The great historical events majestically portrayed in the mosaic seem to welcome us to this chapel. The chapel recalls the baptismal ceremony, the white gown, the burning lamp and the solemn promises made by godmothers and godfathers.

They may be sad memories, the gowns are no longer white, the light of faith has dimmed or perhaps even been extinguished, and we walk in the dark. Promises and commitments have been forgotten.

In this chapel, a moment of silence and meditation can help restore hope and faith in life and in ourselves.

Here, amidst much splendor we can easily recall the words of the Lord, "What is it worth to a man conquer the world if he lose his soul?" This means that our soul is worth more than all the masterpieces in the Basilica.It is even more precious than this final monument, the magnificent baptismal font made of an ancient pale red porphyry cone with a splendid gilded bronze cover (by Fontana) decorated with swirling arabesques and leaves on which we can clearly see the Lamb of God, who "takes away the sins of the world."

Contents